Briefly: Hume's *Dialogues*
Concerning Natural Religion

Briefly: Hume's *Dialogues Concerning Natural Religion*

David Mills Daniel

scm press

The author and publisher acknowledge material reproduced
from R. H. Popkin, ed., *Hume: Dialogues Concerning
Natural Religion*, 2nd edition, Hackett, 1998. Reprinted
by permission of Hackett Publishing Company, Inc.
All rights reserved.

British Library Cataloguing in Publication data

A catalogue record for this book is available
from the British Library

0 334 04025 6/9780 334 04025 5

First published in 2006 by SCM Press
9–17 St Alban's Place,
London N1 0NX

www.scm-canterburypress.co.uk

SCM Press is a division of
SCM-Canterbury Press Ltd

Printed and bound in Great Britain by
CPD (Wales) Ltd, Ebbw Vale

To My Children

Contents

Introduction   ix

Context   1

Who was David Hume?   1
What are the *Dialogues*
   Concerning Natural Religion?   2
Some Issues to Consider   6
Suggestions for Further Reading   7

Detailed Summary of David Hume's
   Dialogues Concerning Natural Religion   9

Pamphilus to Hermippus   9
Part I   10
Part II   12
Part III   16
Part IV   17
Part V   19
Part VI   20
Part VII   21

Contents

Part VIII 23

Part IX 24

Part X 26

Part XI 29

Part XII 32

Overview 37

Glossary 45

Introduction

The SCM *Briefly* series is designed to enable students and general readers to acquire knowledge and understanding of key texts in philosophy, philosophy of religion, theology and ethics. While the series will be especially helpful to those following university and A-level courses in philosophy, ethics and religious studies, it will in fact be of interest to anyone looking for a short guide to the ideas of a particular philosopher or theologian.

Each book in the series takes a piece of work by one philosopher and provides a summary of the original text, which adheres closely to it, and includes direct quotations from it, thus enabling the reader to follow each development in the philosopher's argument(s). Throughout the summary, there are page references to the original philosophical writing, so that the reader has ready access to the primary text. In the Introduction to each book, you will find details of the edition of the philosophical work referred to.

In *Briefly: Hume's Dialogues Concerning Natural Religion*, we refer to David Hume, *Dialogues Concerning Natural Religion*, edited by Richard H. Popkin, second edition, Indianapolis/Cambridge: Hackett Publishing, 1998, ISBN 0872204022.

Each *Briefly* begins with an Introduction, followed by a chapter on the Context in which the work was written. Who was this writer? Why was this book written? With some Issues to Consider, and some Suggested Further Reading, this *Briefly* aims to get anyone started in their philosophical investigation. The detailed summary of the philosophical work is followed by a concise chapter-by-chapter overview and an extensive glossary of terms.

All words that appear in the Glossary are highlighted in bold type the first time that they appear in the Detailed Summary and the Overview of this *Briefly* guide.

Context

Who was David Hume?

David Hume, perhaps the greatest British philosopher, was born in Edinburgh in 1711, and educated at Edinburgh University. He showed an early interest in philosophy, and, after living in France for a time, published his first philosophical work, the *Treatise of Human Nature* (1738–40). It was not particularly well received, but Hume's empirical approach to philosophy meant that he became known as a sceptic and even an atheist. This made him an object of suspicion to the religious and cultural leaders of eighteenth-century Scotland, and may have been a factor in his not being appointed professor of philosophy at Edinburgh University in 1745. Although Hume published further works of philosophy, including *An Enquiry Concerning Human Understanding* (1748) and *An Enquiry Concerning the Principles of Morals* (1751), he turned increasingly to writing about the history of England, which brought him considerable fame. After a period as librarian to the Faculty of Advocates in Edinburgh, Hume was secretary to the British Embassy in Paris, subsequently returning to Scotland, where he died in 1776. In his autobiography, Hume described himself as cheerful, sociable and even-tempered.

What are the *Dialogues Concerning Natural Religion?*

Hume began work on the *Dialogues* in the 1750s. However, the manuscript was not completed until shortly before his death, and was not published until 1779. In view of the book's controversial content, it is not, perhaps, surprising that it was written in dialogue form, making it difficult to identify Hume with the views of any one of the three protagonists. These represent different philosophical positions: Cleanthes, the advocate of natural theology, Philo, the sceptic; and Demea, the defender of religious orthodoxy.

On the face of it, at least, all three protagonists accept that God exists. The issue that they debate, and about which they disagree, is whether or not it is possible for human beings to establish anything about God's nature from their experience of the world. Cleanthes puts forward the design argument. Given the self-evident similarity between the world that God has made and objects made by human beings, we can infer a resemblance between human beings and God. But Philo dissents, pointing out that the similarity between the world, or parts of it, and objects of human design is not so striking that we are entitled to infer similar causes. When we see a house, we know that an architect has designed it, but we have had no experience of the design of worlds, and, therefore, any conclusions we draw about its cause (or, indeed, whether, it has a cause) go beyond our experience. Another way of interpreting the point Philo is making is that not everyone sees the world as having the character of being designed. So far from being a self-evident feature of the world, as Cleanthes claims, it indicates a particular, theistic way of looking at the world.

Cleanthes points to specific features of the world, in particular the eye, as being undeniably designed. But particular examples do not help his case. If (Philo responds) God is the designer, and thus the cause of the world, why are we entitled to say that the world needs a cause and a designer, but God does not? And, focusing specifically on the issue of God's nature, even if the analogy between the world and an object of human design is accepted, the many defects in the world mean that we cannot infer, from our experience of it alone, that God is perfect (we would expect a perfect God to have designed a perfect world), or even that it was designed by only one God, rather than several working together. Philo makes the telling point that it is all too easy (and very tempting) to conclude that, because the world operates in an orderly and predictable way, it must be designed. But, unless it operated predictably, it simply would not be a stable, inhabitable environment at all. And there is no need to conclude that the world's stability must have been caused by God. A much simpler and more economical explanation is that the world is governed by an inherent principle of order. He goes on to argue that Cleanthes is displaying an unjustified bias in favour of the causal principle of intelligent design, as shown by his original analogy between the world and a human-designed object. The world resembles an animal or a vegetable as much as a machine, suggesting generation or vegetation, rather than intelligent design, as its cause.

Apart from agreeing with Philo about the limitations of human reason, the religiously orthodox Demea has played little part in the debate. He now interjects with the opinion that, in view of the inadequacy of Cleanthes' arguments from experience (which Philo has so thoroughly demolished), it is better to use *a priori* ones, which can demonstrate God's existence. Those he chooses: that everything must have a cause, so the universe must have a first cause, God, who cannot be thought not to exist, are swiftly despatched by Cleanthes. There is no

3

being, including God, whose non-existence implies a contra-diction, so God can be thought of as non-existent; but, anyway, this kind of argument could be applied as easily to the universe as to God. And, even if we accept that everything must have a cause, there is no necessity to look for a cause of the series of causes as whole (the universe), as opposed to the individual events within the series.

Demea then argues that it is human misery that makes people turn to God. Philo agrees, raising the problem of evil. How is it possible to infer God's perfections, in particular his benevolence, from our experience of the world, given the presence in it of natural and moral evil? Cleanthes rejects, as mere speculation, Demea's defence that present suffering will be rectified in a future world, but, because he is limited to what (he claims) can be known about God from our experi-ence of the world, he cannot, in responding to Philo's chal-lenge, turn to Christian teaching, and use Christian theodicy to explain why an infinitely powerful and benevolent God allows suffering in the world he created. He cannot argue that providing a pleasant environment for human beings may not have been God's only intention in designing the world, or that suffering, though appalling, may yet fulfil part of God's purpose for human beings.

Therefore, he has to accept Philo's point that we would expect an infinitely powerful and benevolent God to have provided a comfortable world for his creatures to live in. However, he insists that the world contains more pleasure than pain, and claims that, in spite of the suffering it does contain, it is still possible to infer the existence of a finitely powerful and bene-volent God from our experience of it. But, as Philo points out, it is impossible to quantify the balance of happiness and misery in the world, and even if we could, there is still the question of why a finitely perfect God would permit any misery. Suffering is compatible with the existence of a benevolent God, but its presence in the world makes it impossible to prove that such a God exists solely from our experience of it.

At this point, we might expect Philo to be celebrating his victory. Instead, in the final part of the *Dialogues*, he executes a volte-face, accepting that there is evidence of design in nature. However, he only admits that there is some resemblance between the cause of the world and human intelligence, which would not allow natural theology to support much of a religious belief structure. He also claims that being a sceptic is an important step towards Christian belief, because the sceptic recognizes the limitations of human reason, and hence the central importance of revelation for learning anything about God. While it is possible to take this at its face value, perhaps Hume was blunting the edge of Philo's triumph, in order to make the *Dialogues* less offensive to some readers. Even the sceptical Philo pays lip service to the design argument and natural theology, while also putting in a word for revelation. Philo also warns against the possible excesses of popular religion, which is unable to accept that God values virtuous conduct in his followers more than anything else, and applauds the wisdom of societies that keep political power away from religious leaders.

But, whatever the purpose of the final part of the *Dialogues*, Philo has shown that the design argument cannot be used to prove either God's nature or his existence. The narrator, Pamphilus, claims victory for Cleanthes, and it is possible to debate the issue of which of the three protagonists represents Hume's position. However, it is hard to deny that he gives Philo most of the best arguments.

Some Issues to Consider

- The arguments Philo uses to show why the design argument cannot be used to prove anything about God's nature also apply to attempts to use it to prove God's existence.
- We are almost instinctively inclined to regard the fact that the world is a stable environment as suggesting design, and (as Cleanthes urges) to see some of its features, such as the eye, as exhibiting designedness. But, this does not prove anything about God's existence or nature.
- Cleanthes is unable to use Christian teaching to support his case, because he is limited to what (he claims) human beings can know about God from their experience of the world.
- Although the *Dialogues* show that the traditional arguments for the existence of God do not work as proofs of God's existence (they do not offer compelling reasons for an atheist to become a theist), this does not mean that they have no value. If someone is already inclined to see the world as designed, the design argument may help to clarify thinking about the relationship between God and the world.
- While Philo's arguments show why the problem of evil rules out any possibility of proving God's existence and nature solely from our experience of the world, it does not prove (as Philo acknowledges) that God does not exist, or even that God is not benevolent. There may be reasons why God allows evil and suffering in the world: for example, to develop human compassion.
- The question of which of the protagonists (most closely) represents Hume is hard to settle conclusively, but Philo seems to win all the arguments. Philo's volte-face, in the

final part, may just be an attempt to confuse the issue, but Hume may also be making the serious point that, if natural theology cannot tell us anything substantial about God, revelation is the only source of knowledge.

- Hume puts into the mouth of Philo what seem to have been genuine concerns about the nature and effects of what he calls 'popular religion', with its emphasis on fear of God and divine punishment.

Suggestions for Further Reading

David Hume, *Dialogues Concerning Natural Religion*, ed. R. H. Popkin, 2nd edn, Indianapolis/Cambridge: Hackett Publishing Company, 1998.

David Hume, *An Enquiry Concerning Human Understanding*, ed. T. L. Beauchamp, Oxford and New York: Oxford University Press, 1999.

David Hume, *An Enquiry Concerning the Principles of Morals*, ed. J. B. Stewart, 2nd edn, Illinois: Open Court Publishing, 1966.

David Hume, *A Natural History of Religion*, ed. H. E. Root, Stanford: Stanford University Press, 1957.

David Hume, *A Treatise of Human Nature*, ed. E. C. Mossner, London: Penguin, 1969.

A. J. Ayer, *Hume, A Very Short Introduction*, Oxford and New York: Oxford University Press, 2000.

J. C. A. Gaskin, *Hume's Philosophy of Religion*, 2nd edn, London: Macmillan, 1988.

J. H. Hick, *Philosophy of Religion*, 4th edn, Englewood Cliffs, NJ: Prentice-Hall, 1990.

E. C. Mossner, *The Life of David Hume*, 2nd edn, Oxford and New York: Oxford University Press, 1980.

P. Vardy, *The Puzzle of God*, revd edn, London: Fount Paper-
backs, 1999.

Detailed Summary of David Hume's
Dialogues Concerning Natural Religion

Pamphilus To Hermippus (pp. 1–2)

The narrator, **Pamphilus**, writes to his friend, **Hermippus**, to explain that, although the **dialogue** form of treating philosophical issues has gone out of fashion, because it is difficult to handle, tends to 'convey the image of *pedagogue* and *pupil*', and involves sacrificing brevity and precision, in order to preserve 'balance among the speakers', it is suited to certain subjects (p. 1). With points of **doctrine** that are obvious and important, but need to be repeated often, it provides a novel way of dealing with a familiar subject, while it also makes possible a balanced discussion of '*obscure* and *uncertain*' philosophical questions, about which '**human reason** can reach no fixed determination' (p. 1). It is, therefore, a particularly appropriate form for the 'subject of *NATURAL RELIGION*', which brings together the 'obvious' truth of **God**'s existence, the 'only principle which ought never to be a moment absent from our thoughts', and obscure and disputed, but 'so interesting', questions about God's '**attributes**' (p. 1).

Pamphilus, **Cleanthes'** pupil, had been present when these matters were discussed by Cleanthes, the 'accurate' **philosopher**, **Philo**, the 'careless' **sceptic** and **Demea**, whose position was one of 'rigid inflexible **orthodoxy**'; and, to satisfy

Hermippus' curiosity about these conversations, he is providing him with a detailed account of 'their reasonings' (p. 1).

Part I (pp. 3–12)

When Pamphilus joins Cleanthes, Philo and Demea, they discuss his education. Demea expresses the view that, as 'natural theology' is a very difficult subject, requiring the 'maturest judgment', it should be one of the last things that students of **philosophy** learn about (p. 3). Philo expresses surprise that Demea has not taught his children 'the principles of religion' at an earlier stage, but Demea distinguishes between inculcating 'reverence' for these, which he did from the outset, and philosophical discussion of them (p. 3). Starting the latter too soon can result in children becoming arrogant, and rejecting 'established doctrines and opinions' (p. 4). Philo appears to agree with Demea's approach. Philosophy can inspire 'pride and self-sufficiency', which undermines religious belief (p. 4). Indeed, it is important to make clear to students 'the narrow limits of human reason' (p. 4). Given the near impossibility of resolving such philosophical issues as '**cause** and **effect**, extension, space, time, motion', how can human reason be capable of deciding such a matter as 'the origin of worlds' (p. 4)?

Demea is pleased with Philo's observations, but Pamphilus feels that Cleanthes does not take them at their face value. Cleanthes asks Philo if he proposes 'to erect religious **faith** on philosophical skepticism', thinking that, 'if certainty or evidence be expelled from every other subject of inquiry, it will all retire to these theological doctrines, and there acquire a superior force and authority' (p. 5). But how 'absolute and sincere' is Philo's, or anyone else's, professed skepticism

(p. 5)? Even the 'ancient **Pyrrhonians**' found it difficult to be consistently sceptical (p. 5). Like the **Stoics**, they made the error of believing that 'what a man can perform sometimes . . . he can perform always' (p. 6). But, just as the Stoics were mistaken in believing that a sense of duty could always prevail, despite 'pain and sufferings', so too, although somebody might completely renounce all accepted beliefs and opinions, it would be impossible for him to 'persevere in this total skepticism or make it appear in his conduct for a few hours. External objects press in upon him . . . [he] will not be able . . . to preserve the poor appearance of skepticism' (p. 5).

However, Philo argues that, although the most determined sceptic 'must act . . . and live, and converse' like everybody else, if he has 'accustomed himself to skeptical considerations on the uncertainty and narrow limits of reason, he will not entirely forget them when he turns his reflection on other subjects' (p. 6). And such scepticism is particularly important with subjects that go 'beyond human affairs', such as '**theological reasonings**' about, for example, 'the **creation** and formation of the **universe**' (p. 7).

Cleanthes claims that, whatever the sceptics may say, their 'doctrine and practice' are always at odds with one another (p. 8). Even with the most '**abstruse points of theory**', they abandon their scepticism, once confronted by evidence (p. 8). Indeed, persistent scepticism is an enemy to knowledge as well as religion, and would involve rejection of the theories of **Newton**, **Copernicus** and **Galileo**. And, just as sceptics 'proportion their assent to the precise degree of evidence' in mathematics and science, they should do the same with 'theological and religious' questions (p. 9). Indeed, unlike the Copernican system, which appears 'contrary to . . . our very senses', religious **hypotheses** are often based on the 'simplest and most obvious arguments' (p. 10).

For centuries (Cleanthes continues), it had been the practice of **Christian** leaders and teachers to elevate faith at the expense of reason, and to decry 'every principle derived merely from human research and inquiry' (p. 10). In fact, **Locke** had been the first Christian to maintain that: '*faith* was nothing but a species of *reason*; that religion was only a branch of philosophy; and that a chain of arguments, similar to that which established any truth in morals, politics, or physics, was always employed in discovering all the principles of **theology**, natural and **revealed**' (pp. 10–11). Philo does not dissent. In '**ignorant ages**', priests had believed that 'presumptuous questioning of **received opinions**' could lead to **atheism**, but even their views had now changed: 'If we distrust human reason we have now no other principle to lead us into religion' (pp. 11–12).

Cleanthes is convinced that it is the use of reason that will 'tend to the confirmation of true religion, and serve to confound the **cavils** of atheists, **libertines**, and **free thinkers**' (p. 12).

Part II (pp. 13–22)

Demea believes that, while no one 'ever entertained a serious doubt' about the '**self-evident**' truth of God's existence, nothing can be known about his **nature**, due to the 'infirmities of human understanding' (p. 13). Thus, his 'attributes, the manner of his existence, the very nature of his duration . . . are mysterious to men. **Finite**, weak and blind **creatures**, we ought to humble ourselves in his august presence' (p. 13).

Philo agrees: 'Our ideas reach no farther than our **experience**. We have no experience of **divine** attributes and operations. I need not conclude my **syllogism**: You can draw the **inference** yourself' (p. 15). For him, God is something that exists with the **attribute** of being the cause of the universe:

'Nothing exists without a cause; and the original cause of this universe (whatever it be) we call *God*, and **piously** ascribe to him every species of **perfection**' (p. 14). Beyond this, however, he does not think it is possible to advance. He warns that, as 'all perfection is entirely relative', human beings should never imagine that they 'comprehend the attributes of this divine Being', or think that his 'perfections have any **analogy** or likeness to the perfections of a human creature' (p. 14). Such words as 'Wisdom, thought, **design**, knowledge' are justly ascribed to him, because they are 'honourable among men', who lack other words and concepts to express their 'adoration of him' (p. 14). But it is important to recognize that such ideas do not 'anywise correspond to his perfections'; nor do 'his attributes have any resemblance to these qualities among men' (p. 14).

But it is precisely this sort of enterprise that Cleanthes wants to undertake, and he delivers an eloquent statement of the evidence of design in the **world**, 'the whole and every part' of which is 'nothing but one great machine, subdivided into an **infinite** number of lesser machines' (p. 15). These machines are all '**adjusted** to each other with an accuracy which **ravishes** into admiration all men', while the ingenious 'adapting of means to ends, throughout all nature, resembles exactly, though it much exceeds, the productions of human **contrivance**; of human design, thought, wisdom, and intelligence' (p. 15). As the 'effects resemble each other, we are led to infer, by all the rules of analogy, that the causes also resemble' (p. 15). Therefore, the '**Author** of Nature' resembles the **mind** of man, but possesses: 'much larger **faculties**, proportioned to the grandeur of the work which he has executed' (p. 15). It is only by such an 'argument *a posteriori*' that we can 'prove at once the existence of a **Deity** and his similarity to human mind and intelligence' (p. 15).

Demea opposes Cleanthes' argument: 'I could not approve of your conclusion concerning the similarity of the Deity to men; still less can I approve of the **mediums** by which you endeavor to establish it. What! No **demonstration** of the **Being of God**! No **abstract arguments**! No proofs *a priori!* ... Can we reach no further ... than experience and probability?' (p. 15). However, it is left to Philo to demolish Cleanthes' argument. He points out that the less similar any two cases are, the weaker any analogy between them is likely to be, and challenges Cleanthes' analogy between items made by human beings, which we know to have been the creation of a mind, and the universe. If we see a house, we can conclude with certainty that it had an **architect**, because 'this is precisely that species of effect which we have experienced to proceed from this species of cause' (p. 16). But it cannot be affirmed that 'the universe bears such a resemblance to a house that we can with the same certainty infer a similar cause, or that the analogy here is entire and perfect' (p. 16). As the differences between the two are 'so striking', the most that can be claimed is 'a guess, a **conjecture**, a presumption concerning a similar cause' (p. 16).

Cleanthes disagrees. He is not putting forward a 'guess or conjecture' (p. 16). Is the resemblance between 'the whole **adjustment** of means to ends in a house and in the universe' really so slight? (p. 16). But, for Philo, the resemblance is not close enough to warrant any conclusion. If somebody could close his eyes, and 'abstract' himself from everything he knows or has seen, he could not work out, from his own ideas alone, what the universe is like (p. 17). Similarly, if he then opened his eyes, and observed the world, he would be unable to decide its cause. His imagination could run riot, and throw up all sorts of possibilities: 'but, being all equally possible, he would never of himself give a satisfactory account for his preferring one of them to the rest' (p. 17). Only experience can point out 'the true cause of any phenomenon' (p. 17). The features of the world to which Cleanthes has pointed, such as 'order, arrangement, or the adjustment of final causes', do not prove design, unless they have been 'experienced to proceed from that principle' (p. 17). But for all we 'can know *a priori*, **matter** may contain the source or spring of order originally within itself, as well as mind does' (pp. 17–18). Cleanthes has compared 'houses, ships, furniture, machines' to the universe, and, 'from their similarity in some circumstances, inferred a similarity in their causes' (p. 19). However, 'thought, design, intelligence', as found in men and animals, are only 'one of the **springs and principles** of the universe' (p. 19). True, it is 'an active cause', by which some 'parts of nature' produce changes in 'other parts', but can a conclusion legitimately be 'transferred from parts to the whole' (p. 19)? And, if the effects of one part of nature on another is to become the basis of 'our judgment concerning the *origin* of the whole', why should 'peculiar privilege' be given to 'this little agitation of the brain' (p. 19)? Why should thought be made 'the **model of the whole universe**' (p. 19)? Even if thought, resembling that of human beings, exists throughout the universe, there may also be 'new and unknown principles' that 'actuate' nature (p. 20). Where 'two species of objects' have always been observed as '**conjoined** together', experience entitles us to infer the existence of one from that of the other (p. 20). But this argument does not apply where the objects are 'single, individual, without parallel' (p. 21). To be entitled to claim that 'an orderly universe must arise from some thought and **art** like the human', we would need experience of 'the origin of worlds' (p. 21).

Cleanthes interrupts to say that Philo's arguments could be used to challenge 'the *Copernican* system' (p. 21). We have not seen other earths moving. However, Philo points out that we have: the moon and all the planets. Thus, while the conclusions of astronomers were based on evidence, the subject that Cleanthes is pursuing 'exceeds all human reason and inquiry' (p. 22). Is Cleanthes really able to maintain that he can show any 'similarity between the fabric of a house and the generation of a universe' (p. 22)?

Part III (pp. 23–7)

However, Cleanthes maintains that there is no necessity to prove the similarity of '**works of nature** to those of art', because such similarity is 'self-evident and undeniable' (p. 23). He invites Philo to imagine that there was a universal language and that books were 'natural productions', which perpetuated themselves like animals and vegetables (p. 24). When Philo referred to these 'natural volumes containing the most refined reason' in his library, he could hardly doubt that their 'original cause bore the strongest analogy to mind and intelligence' (p. 24). Yet the 'anatomy of an animal' showed more evidence of design than such books (p. 25). So, Philo must either assert that such books would not be 'proof of a rational cause', or concede that there is a 'similar cause to all the works of nature' (p. 25). He then takes the example of the eye, and asks Philo to consider its 'structure and contrivance'. Does not the 'idea of a contriver' strike him 'with a force like that of sensation' (p. 25). Confronted by 'millions' of such examples, what degree of 'blind **dogmatism** must one have attained to reject such natural and such convincing arguments?' (p. 25).

At this point, it is Demea who challenges Cleanthes, accusing him of being 'presumptuous', by 'making us imagine we comprehend the Deity and have some adequate idea of his nature and attributes' (p. 26). He feels that Cleanthes' line of argument, by emphasizing the similarities of God to the human mind, makes human beings 'the model of the whole universe' (p. 27). It is also 'unreasonable' to believe that human emotions, which reflect the 'state and situation of man', apply to God (p. 27).

Part IV (pp. 28–33)

Cleanthes concedes that God has 'powers and attributes' that exceed human comprehension, but accuses Demea of being a **mystic** (p. 28). If human beings' ideas of God, 'so far as they go, be not just and adequate and correspondent to his real nature, I know not what there is in this subject worth insisting on' (p. 28). But Demea has a point. What he calls Cleanthes' '*anthropomorphite*' approach, of representing 'the Deity as similar to a human mind and understanding', is not straightforward (p. 28). How are the distinct faculties, and ever-changing ideas and feelings, of the human mind similar to, or compatible with, 'that perfect **immutability** and **simplicity** which all true **theists** ascribe to the Deity' (p. 29)?

Cleanthes counters this point by arguing that those who maintain the 'perfect simplicity of the **Supreme Being**' are '*atheists*' as well as '*mystics*' (p. 29). Although 'the Deity possesses attributes of which we have no comprehension', we should not ascribe to him those that are 'absolutely incompatible with that intelligent nature essential to him' (p. 29). A 'wholly simple and totally immutable' mind, without thought, reason or will, would be 'no mind at all' (p. 29).

Philo reproves Cleanthes: he is now calling all 'orthodox divines' atheists (p. 29). He also points out the 'inconveniences' of Cleanthes' 'anthropomorphism' (p. 30). Reason suggests that a '**mental world** or universe' requires a cause as much as a '**material world** or **universe of objects**' (p. 30). Even if it is admitted that the universe is caused by a mind, there is a need to postulate a further cause: of this mind. But that cause would require another cause, and so on, '*in infinitum*' (p. 31). It would be both more sensible and more economical to suppose that 'the principle of its order' lay in the universe itself, and thus 'assert it to be God' than to hold that it requires God to cause it, but, at the same time, to maintain that God requires no cause (p. 31). To claim that 'the different ideas which compose the reason of the Supreme Being fall into order of themselves and by their own nature is really to talk without any precise meaning' (p. 31). If it does mean anything, then why does it not make as much sense to say that 'the parts of the material world fall into order of themselves and by their own nature' (p. 31)? We have experience of ideas that 'fall into order of themselves and without any *known* cause' (p. 31). However, we have more experience of 'matter which does the same' (p. 31). When the question is asked: 'what cause produces order in the ideas of the Supreme Being, can any other reason by assigned by you, anthropomorphites, than that it is a *rational* faculty, and that such is the nature of the Deity?' (p. 32). In which case, why is a similar answer not 'satisfactory in accounting for the order of the world' (p. 32)?

Cleanthes is unimpressed. In everyday life, when a cause is assigned to an event, it may be the case that the cause of that cause cannot be assigned. For him, the 'order and arrange-ment of Nature, the **curious** adjustment of final causes' point clearly to '**an intelligent cause or author**' (p. 32). In fact, heaven and the earth 'join in the same testimony: The whole chorus of Nature raises one hymn to the praises of its **Creator**', and, having found God, he will end his enquiry (pp. 32–3). However,

Philo contends that, while it is legitimate to explain particular effects by general causes that remain inexplicable, this is not so where, as in the case of the universe and God, an attempt is being made to explain 'a particular effect' (the universe) by 'a particular cause' (God), which is 'no more to be accounted for than the effect itself' (p. 33).

Part V (pp. 34–8)

Philo points out 'more inconveniences' of Cleanthes' anthropomorphic approach (p. 34). '*Like effects prove like causes*', so the more alike the effects that are seen, and the causes inferred, 'the stronger is the argument' (p. 34). Scientific discovery is forever unveiling new aspects of the 'grandeur and magnificence' of the universe, and these should provide further arguments in support of God's powers (p. 34). But for Cleanthes, they become obstacles, because they show how unlike humans God must be. We are 'led to infer the **universal cause** of all to be vastly different from mankind' (p. 35). Indeed, Cleanthes' analogical reasoning imposes strict limits on what can be known about God. It precludes 'all claim to infinity in any of the attributes of the Deity', because cause must be in proportion to effect, and what we know of the effect is not infinite (p. 35). Similarly, perfection cannot be ascribed to God, because of the many **defects** in nature. These would not be a problem if God's perfect nature had been established by *a priori* arguments, because then they would just be a puzzle for the limited intellectual capacity of human beings, who cannot comprehend the mind of God. It would just have to be accepted that the world is as it is for good reasons, which human beings just do not understand. But if the effect, the world with all its defects, is put forward as the only basis upon which to establish knowledge of God's nature, it is impossible to know whether it 'contains any great faults or deserves any considerable praise if compared to other possible and even real systems' (p. 36).

However, even if the world were perfect, how could we know, on the basis of our knowledge of the world alone, whether this was to the credit of the divine 'workman' (p. 36)? We might be full of admiration for a ship, but then find that it has been made by a 'stupid **mechanic**', who copied the work of others (p. 36). Many worlds might have been 'botched and bungled' before the present one was produced (p. 36). And how can we tell that it is the work of only one God? Many men co-operate to build ships and houses. Why should not 'several deities' have joined together to make the world (p. 36)? Philo goes on to give full rein to his imagination. From what we can infer of God from the world, he might be '**corporeal**'; the world might have been the first botched effort of an 'infant deity'; or the last, weak product of a 'superannuated' one (p. 37).

However, Cleanthes is not disconcerted by Philo's arguments, which only show that he can 'never get rid of the hypothesis of design in the universe' (p. 38).

Part VI (pp. 39–43)

Philo returns to the basis of Cleanthes' theological reasoning: the principle that 'like effects arise from like causes' (p. 39). But there is another relevant principle: that 'where several known circumstances are *observed* to be similar, the unknown will also be *found* similar' (p. 39). The world seems to resemble an animal more than 'works of human art and contrivance', so why should not the world be 'an animal' and God, 'the **Soul** of the world' (p. 40)? Cleanthes, he maintains, cannot reject this view by arguing that our limited experience is 'an unequal standard by which to judge of the unlimited extent of nature', because he has insisted that experience must be the 'only guide' in **'theological inquiries'** (p. 40). If he took this route, he would have to 'abandon' his hypothesis, and 'adopt our mysticism' (p. 40).

Cleanthes unwisely responds by saying that, although the world may resemble an animal, it bears a closer resemblance to a vegetable, a point that Philo picks up later. At this point, Philo insists that, if any explanation of the world had to be defended, the most plausible is one that ascribes to it 'an eternal, **inherent** principle of order . . . How could things have been as they are, were there not an original inherent principle of order somewhere, in thought or in matter' (pp. 42–3). Instead of marvelling at the fact that there is order in the world, it should be recognized that any alternative is 'absolutely impossible' (p. 43). For the world to be a stable and habitable environment, it has to operate according to 'steady, **inviolable laws'** (p. 43).

Part VII (pp. 44–8)

Philo returns to the view that the world resembles an animal or a vegetable more than 'the works of human art' (p. 44). If so, 'it is more probable that its cause resembles the cause of the former than the latter', so that its 'origin ought rather to be ascribed to generation or vegetation than to reason or design' (p. 44). Cleanthes had claimed that experience alone could decide questions about the Deity, and that, on this basis, the world most resembled 'works of human contrivance', so its cause must resemble a human mind (p. 44). But Cleanthes had selected 'the operation of one very small part of nature', that of human beings on inanimate matter, as the criterion for determining the origin of the universe as a whole (p. 44). But, as the world was more like 'an animal or a vegetable' than 'a watch or a **knitting-loom**', so its origin was more likely to be generation or vegetation (p. 44).

Demea objects that there is no evidence for 'such extraordinary conclusions', as the resemblance of the world to an animal or vegetable is so slight (p. 45). Philo agrees wholeheartedly. That is exactly his point. There is 'no *data* to establish any system of **cosmogony**', because of the imperfect and limited nature of human experience, which can provide no 'probable conjecture' about the nature and origins of the universe as a whole (p. 45). So one hypothesis is as good as another. As far as human experience goes, there are 'four principles, *reason, instinct, generation, vegetation*', which produce 'similar effects' (p. 46). Any one of these could account for the origin of the universe. Cleanthes had confined his hypothesis to reason, the one by which human minds operate. But any claim that order in animals and vegetables 'proceeds ultimately from design is begging the question' (p. 47). Such a claim could not be proved on the basis of our experience of the world, but only by 'proving, *a priori*' that order is 'inseparably attached to thought', and can never 'of itself or from original unknown principles belong to matter' (p. 47). Further, judging by 'our limited and imperfect experience, generation has some privileges above reason. For we see every day the latter arise from the former, never the former from the latter' (p. 47). He claims that the world resembles an animal, and arose from generation; Cleanthes that it resembles a machine, and arose from design. 'The steps are . . . equally wide' in both arguments, but Cleanthes' analogy is 'less striking' (p. 47). Indeed, a case could be made for the **Brahmin** hypothesis that the world was produced by an infinite spider; and why should it not be 'spun from the belly as well as from the brain' (p. 48)?

Cleanthes is able only to admire Philo's inventiveness: his 'whimsies . . . may puzzle but never can convince us' (p. 48).

Part VIII (pp. 49–53)

Philo defends himself against Cleanthes' accusation of fertile 'invention' (p. 49). As far as the origin of the world is concerned, 'a hundred contradictory views' could be consistent with our experience of it, and may 'preserve a kind of imperfect analogy' (p. 49). An **'unknown voluntary agent'** was merely one 'hypothesis attended with no advantages. The beginning of motion in matter itself is as conceivable *a priori* as its communication from mind and intelligence' (p. 50). Indeed, wherever, as is the case with the world, 'matter is so poised, arranged and adjusted, as to continue in **perpetual motion**, and yet preserve a **constancy in the forms,** its situation must, of necessity, have all the same appearance of art and contrivance which we observe at present' (p. 50). All 'the parts of each form have a relation to each other and to the whole', and, where defects in the system arise, 'chaos ensues' until forms emerge, 'whose parts and organs are so adjusted as to support the forms amidst a continued succession of matter'; but the overall stability of 'the present world' suggests design (pp. 50–1). And it is all very well to point to 'the uses of the parts in animals or vegetables, and their curious adjustment to each other'; but, given the nature of the world, and, therefore, the kind of environment in which they have to survive, how could any animal 'subsist unless its parts were so adjusted? Do we not find that it immediately perishes whenever this adjustment ceases' (p. 51)?

Cleanthes' response is to argue that Philo's theory does not take account of 'the many conveniences and advantages which men and all animals possess': two eyes and ears, rather than only one; the availability to human beings of animals and fruits, which are useful, or give enjoyment, but which are not essential to their survival; and so on (p. 52). Any one of these is: 'a sufficient proof of design, and of a **benevolent** design, which gave rise to the order and arrangement of the universe' (p. 52).

But Philo insists that Cleanthes' anthropomorphism leads him to give 'thought the precedence' (p. 52). He reminds him that our experience of the world shows that: 'thought has no influence upon matter except where that matter is so conjoined with it as to have an equal reciprocal influence upon it' (pp. 52–3).

Part IX (pp. 54–7)

At this point, Demea intervenes. As *a posteriori* arguments create so many difficulties, why not depend on *a priori* ones? These also make it possible to prove the infinity of God's attributes and the **unity of the divine nature**, which cannot be **deduced** from 'contemplating the works of Nature' (p. 54). Whatever exists must have 'a cause or reason of its existence', so, unless we are prepared to go on 'in tracing an **infinite succession**' of causes, we 'must at last have recourse to some **ultimate cause** that is *necessarily* **existent**', who 'carries the *reason* of his existence in himself; and who cannot be supposed not to exist, without an express **contradiction**' (pp. 54–5). Consequently, there is 'such a Being – that is, there is a Deity' (p. 55).

It is Cleanthes who points out the weaknesses of this

'**metaphysical reasoning**' (p. 55). First, it is absurd to try to demonstrate a matter of fact by *a priori* arguments. Nothing is 'demonstrable unless the contrary implies a contradiction' (p. 55). Whatever we **conceive** as existent, we can 'also conceive as non-existent' (p. 55). Therefore, there is 'no being . . . whose non-existence implies a contradiction. Consequently there is no being whose existence is demonstrable' (p. 55). It may be claimed that God is a necessarily existent being, and that we would see that it is impossible for him not to exist if we knew his 'whole **essence** or nature'; but we are not going to do so, given our limited faculties (p. 55). And our minds are not under the necessity of 'supposing any object to remain always in being; in the same manner as we lie under a necessity of always conceiving twice two to be four' (p. 55). So, the words '"**necessary existence**" have no meaning' (pp. 55–6).

Further, Demea's argument provided no reason for concluding that God, rather than the 'material universe', was 'necessarily existent', or that the universe did not contain qualities which, if we knew of them, would make its non-existence seem as much of a contradiction as two and two making five (p. 56). It was argued that matter and 'the form of the world' were **contingent**, and could be conceived as being 'annihilated' or 'altered' (p. 56). But the same argument could be applied to God: the mind could conceive of him as non-existent and/or his attributes altered. Again, in a succession of objects, each one is caused by the preceding one, which causes the next. What was the problem with this? Why was a cause of the whole succession needed?: 'Did I show you the particular causes of each individual in a collection of twenty particles of matter, I should think it very unreasonable should you afterwards ask me what was the cause of the whole twenty. This is sufficiently explained in explaining the cause of the parts' (p. 56).

Philo adds that *a priori* arguments, like Demea's, only convince those 'of a metaphysical head', who have found that, in mathematics, 'understanding frequently leads to truth through obscurity', and who have 'transferred the same habit of thinking to subjects where it ought not to have place' (p. 57).

Part X (pp. 58–66)

Demea then suggests that each individual feels 'the truth of religion', as a result of his own experience of misery, rather than through reasoning: 'Necessity, hunger, want stimulate the strong and courageous; fear, anxiety, terror agitate the weak and infirm' (pp. 58–9). Philo agrees: both the 'learned' and the **'vulgar'** concur on 'the topic of human misery' (p. 58). Indeed, human beings' intelligence, capacity for reflection and ability to organize themselves make their misery greater than that of animals. They have 'become master of the whole animal creation', but their lives are ruined by the *'imaginary* enemies' of fear and anxiety (p. 60). Furthermore, 'Man is the greatest enemy of man'; human beings are always finding ways to 'mutually torment each other' (p. 60). Society, which enables human beings to overcome the 'wild beasts, his natural enemies', exposes them to such ills as oppression, injustice violence, war and fraud, which would soon dissolve society, 'were it not for the dread of still greater ills' (p. 61).

Even worse, according to Demea, are the 'disorders of the mind', which afflict human beings, such as remorse, rage, disappointment and despair (p. 61). While all of life's good things would not make a 'very happy man', all its ills would 'make a wretch indeed' (p. 62). Evidence of human misery is to be found everywhere. If a stranger were to drop in on the world suddenly, he would show him, 'as a specimen of its ills, a hospital full of diseases, a prison crowded with **malefactors** and **debtors**, a field of battle strewed with carcasses, a fleet foundering in the ocean' (p. 61). And the supposedly cheerful 'side of life' would be no better: 'a ball . . . an opera . . . court? He might justly think that I was only showing him a diversity of distress and sorrow' (p. 61).

Cleanthes dissents, expressing the hope that such unhappiness is not 'so common' as Demea and Philo claim (p. 62). However, Demea insists that even the most favoured, such as the rich and powerful, experience 'human misery' (p. 62). Cleanthes should ask himself whether anyone he knew would really wish to 'live over again the last ten or twenty years of their life' (p. 62). Philo then teases Cleanthes. Can Cleanthes, in the face of all this evidence, still persevere in his anthropomorphism, asserting that 'the moral attributes of the Deity, his justice, benevolence, mercy and rectitude' are of 'the same nature with these virtues in human creatures' (p. 63)? God's power and wisdom are 'infinite', while he is 'never mistaken in choosing the means to any end' (p. 63). In which case, why does the course of nature not tend to 'human or animal **felicity** . . . In what respect then do his benevolence and mercy resemble the benevolence and mercy of men' (p. 63)?

Philo repeats **Epicurus'** question:

Is he willing to prevent evil, but not able? then he is **impotent**. Is he able, but not willing? then he is **malevolent**. Is he both able and willing? whence then is evil? (p. 63)

Cleanthes may claim that nature has a purpose, but its only one is the '**preservation** alone **of individuals**, and **propagation of the species**' (p. 63).

Cleanthes acknowledges the importance of the issue. If Philo can show that human beings are 'unhappy or **corrupted**', that is the 'end at once of all religion' (p. 64). Demea does not accept this point. This world may be full of misery, but the situation will be put right 'in some future period of existence' (p. 64). But this will not do for Cleanthes. How can 'any cause be known but from its known effects' (p. 64)? Thus, talk of **future worlds** is just so much speculation. There is only one 'method of supporting divine benevolence', which is, 'to deny absolutely the misery and wickedness of man' (p. 64). Overall: 'Health is more common than sickness: Pleasure than pain: Happiness than misery' (p. 65).

Philo, however, contends that, even if there is less pain than pleasure, it has a much bigger effect on our lives, and can, in fact, dominate and destroy them. He also insists that Cleanthes has, from his own point of view, put the debate on 'a most dangerous issue' (p. 65). He has committed himself to the position that there is no 'just foundation for religion', unless the happiness of human life is established (p. 65). But how could the balance between pleasure and pain, in the lives of all humans and animals, ever be calculated? Cleanthes' whole religious system hinges on a point that can never be determined either way. What is more, even if there is more happiness than unhappiness in the world, why, if God is infinitely good and powerful, 'is there any misery at all in the world' (p. 66)? Human pain and misery may be *'compatible'* with God's '**infinite power** and goodness', but its presence makes it impossible to prove the existence of these 'pure, unmixed, and uncontrollable' attributes from the 'mixed and confused phenomena' of the world (p. 66). There is no 'view of human life or of the condition of mankind' from which, without great violence, God's 'moral attributes', or his '**infinite benevolence**, conjoined with infinite power and **infinite wisdom'**, can be inferred (p. 66). These must be discovered by 'the eyes of faith alone' (p. 66).

Part XI (pp. 67–76)

Cleanthes picks up on the word 'infinite' (p. 67). Admittedly, if 'we preserve human analogy', it is impossible to reconcile evil in the universe with God's 'infinite attributes'; that is, to prove the existence of such a God from the mixed evidence available in the world (p. 67). But, if God is thought to be only **'finitely perfect** . . . a satisfactory account may then be given of natural and **moral evil'** (p. 67). Philo is not convinced. If someone, unacquainted with the universe, were assured that it was 'the production of a very good, wise and powerful Being, however finite', he would form, before he saw it, 'a different notion of it from what we find it to be by experience' (p. 68). He would certainly not expect it to be 'so full of vice and misery and disorder' (p. 68).

Philo acknowledges that if this person was absolutely convinced, before he saw it, that the universe had been made by such a being, he might not relinquish this conviction, despite all the evil and suffering he found. He might just accept that God had reasons, which will 'for ever escape his comprehension', for allowing their presence (p. 68). But if, as is the case with human beings, they are not **'antecedently** convinced' of the existence of a good and powerful God, they will not, 'from the **appearances** of things' in the universe, conclude that such a being created it, or even that such a being exists (p. 68). If someone looks around a house where nothing fits or works properly, the 'architect would in vain' claim that it had to stay as it was, because, if one part were altered, it would make the house, as a whole, even worse (p. 68). The response would be that, if the architect had had 'skill and good intentions', he would have designed a better house in the first place (p. 68). While the defects of the world may be consistent with the idea of a good and powerful God, no 'inference concerning his existence' can be drawn from the world, because it is 'different from what a man ... would, *beforehand*, expect from a very powerful, wise, and benevolent Deity' (p. 69).

Further, Philo indicates four factors that intensify the ills that humans and animals suffer. The first is that they are moved to action and self-preservation by pain as well as pleasure. But why not just pleasure? Creatures could be 'constantly in a state of enjoyment', which would diminish slightly if they needed to undertake some self-preserving act, such as eating or drinking (p. 69). The second is 'the conducting of the world by **general laws**', which often cause pain and suffering (p. 70). Why could not God have caused the world to operate by 'particular **volitions**', which would turn any potentially damaging or destructive situations or events into beneficial ones, thus making 'the whole world happy', without revealing himself 'in any operation' (p. 70)? For example, fleets with vital cargoes would always have fair winds, while rulers would always have good dispositions, if necessary by having their personalities altered.

The third is 'the great **frugality** with which all powers and faculties are distributed' to humans and animals (p. 71). Their powers may be adequate to their needs, but why do they not exceed them? Why do humans or animals with particular strengths also suffer from 'proportional abatement' in other powers (p. 71)? Animals, capable of speed, are often 'defective in force' (p. 71). Human beings possess 'reason and **sagacity**', but are 'the most deficient in bodily advantages', while their lack of inclination to 'industry and labor' means that they do not improve their lot as much as they might (pp. 71–2). In fact, 'idleness' is the cause of almost 'all the moral as well as **natural evils** of human life'; if human beings were exempt from it, they would soon 'reach that state of society which is so imperfectly attained by the best regulated government' (p. 72).

The fourth is 'the inaccurate workmanship' of the world (p. 73). Winds, vital for navigation, also give rise to storms; rains, essential for cultivation, bring floods; heat is necessary, but also often excessive: 'There is nothing so advantageous in the universe but what frequently becomes pernicious, by its excess or defect' (p. 73).

Some might argue (Philo continues) that these factors are not essential to the universe, and 'might easily have been altered' (p. 74). But he is prepared to be 'more modest' in his conclusions (p. 74). If God's goodness could be established on *a priori* grounds, the world's defects, 'however **untoward**', might be 'reconcilable to it' (p. 74). But there is no possibility of inferring God's goodness from the universe, when it contains 'so many ills' (p. 74). The 'variety and **fecundity**' of the universe may be striking, but so, too, is the mutual hostility and destructiveness of the beings that inhabit it (p. 74). This suggests 'nothing but the idea of a **blind nature**', and a cause with 'no more regard to good above ill than to heat above cold' (pp. 74–5). Nor, according to Philo, can God's goodness be inferred from the existence of human benevolence, as moral evil 'is much more predominant above moral good than natural evil above natural good' (p. 75). But, even if the reverse were the case (he puts it to Cleanthes), 'so long as there is any vice at all in the universe, it will very much puzzle you anthropomorphites how to account for it' (p. 75).

Demea, who, in order to 'prove the **incomprehensible**

nature of the Divine Being', has joined in the attack on Cleanthes' attempts to 'measure everything by human rule and
standard', now sees the implications of Philo's arguments, and
recognizes his scepticism as 'a more dangerous enemy than
Cleanthes himself' (p. 75). Cleanthes reproves Demea for his
failure to perceive the implications of the theological position
he shares with so many 'orthodox divines' (p. 76). Emphasizing the incomprehensibility of God, and the misery of human
existence, may engender 'superstition' in 'ages of stupidity
and ignorance', but they will not work in a more enlightened
era (p. 76). Philo suggests that Demea's approach is actually
out of date. Modern **theologians** recognized the need to 'make
use of such arguments as will endure at least some scrutiny
and examination', and allowed that there were 'more pleasures
than pains, even in this life', as this was more likely to draw
people to belief in God than stressing all life's 'ills and pains'
(p. 76).

At this point, Demea, uncomfortable with the turn the
discussion is taking, makes his excuses and leaves.

Part XII (pp. 77–89)

Philo now acknowledges that 'no one has a deeper sense of
religion impressed on his mind, or pays more profound
adoration to the Divine Being, as he discovers himself to reason
in the inexplicable contrivance and **artifice** of nature' than he
does; and that a 'purpose, an intention, a design strikes everywhere the most careless, the most stupid thinker' (p. 77). He
refers to the example of the human body, and the astonish-
ment we feel 'in proportion to the number and intricacy of the
parts so artificially adjusted' (p. 78). Cleanthes, in response
to what Philo has 'so well urged', reiterates his point that the

'comparison of the universe to a machine of human contrivance is so obvious and natural . . . that it must immediately strike all unprejudiced **apprehensions**, and procure universal approbation' (p. 79). A contrary interpretation of the world 'can never be steadily maintained against such striking appearances as continually engage us into the religious hypothesis' (p. 79).

And Philo appears to agree. Now his point is that, although the works of nature bear 'a great analogy to the productions of art', there are considerable differences, indicating a 'proportional difference in the causes' (p. 79). But whatever we choose to call 'the first and supreme cause', his existence can be 'plainly ascertained by reason' (p. 80). Thus, while the theist acknowledges that 'the **original intelligence** is very different from human reason', even the atheist has to admit that 'the original principle of order bears some remote analogy to it' (p. 81). However, as the 'works of Nature' bear a closer analogy to 'the effects of *our* art and contrivance' than 'those of *our* benevolence and justice', we must infer that God's 'natural attributes' resemble those of human beings more closely than his moral attributes do 'human virtues': which suggests that, as God is 'absolutely and entirely perfect', human beings' 'moral qualities' are more defective than their 'natural abilities' (p. 81). Philo also admits that it is only his 'veneration for true religion' and 'abhorrence of **vulgar superstitions**' that prompts him to push his exploration of religious principles 'sometimes into absurdity, sometimes into impiety' (p. 82).

Cleanthes is less condemnatory of vulgar superstition: even 'corrupted' religion is better than 'no religion at all' (p. 82). The idea of a 'future state' is 'so strong and necessary a security to morals', as the effects on conduct of the 'rewards and punishments', meted out in this life, show (p. 82). Philo disagrees: if 'vulgar superstition' benefits society, why is history full of 'accounts of its pernicious consequences' (p. 82)? References to it always include details of 'the miseries which attend it', such as oppression, persecution and civil war (p. 82). However, Cleanthes considers that, as the function of religion is to 'regulate the hearts of men', and enforce 'morality and justice', its beneficial effects are often 'overlooked and confounded with these other motives' (p. 82). But Philo makes the point that, while theologians and clergy may claim that the power of religious motives makes it 'impossible for civil society to subsist' without them, in reality, unlike human beings' natural inclinations, which work 'incessantly' upon them, religious motives operate only intermittently, so 'it is scarcely possible for them to become altogether habitual to the mind' (p. 83). Further, philosophers and thinkers, who 'cultivate reason', have little need for religious motives to enforce moral behaviour, while 'the vulgar', who do, 'are utterly incapable of so pure a religion as represents the Deity to be pleased with nothing but virtue in human behavior' (p. 84). Indeed, trying to cultivate religious motives can lead to a 'habit of **dissimulation**', which is why 'the highest zeal in religion' is often combined with 'the deepest hypocrisy' (p. 84). If 'vulgar superstition' promoted morality, society would not keep the exercise of political power out of the 'dangerous hands' of priests: 'if the spirit of **popular religion** were so salutary to society, a contrary **maxim** ought to prevail' (p. 85). 'True religion' may have desirable consequences, but we must 'treat of religion as it has commonly been found in the world' (p. 86).

Cleanthes urges Philo not to allow his 'zeal against false religion' to undermine his 'veneration for the true' (p. 91). The 'most agreeable reflection' for human beings is that of 'genuine theism': that we are 'the workmanship of a Being perfectly good, wise and powerful; who created us for happiness' (p. 86).

Part XII (pp. 77–89)

Philo warns that, while this is the case for philosophers, for the majority, 'the **terrors** of religion commonly prevail above its **comforts**' (p. 86). Again, people turn to religion in times of grief and sickness, showing that the 'religious spirit' is allied to sorrow not joy (p. 86). He agrees with Cleanthes that religion can be a '**consolation**', but points out that in 'popular religion', unlike that which results from 'philosophy', the '**damned**' outnumber the '**elect**'; the situation of '**departed souls**', amid 'torrents of **fire and brimstone**', is always portrayed in a way which would never make it 'eligible for human kind that there should be such a state' (p. 87). When people are happy, they engage in social or business activities, and do not think of religion. It is when they are depressed that they 'brood upon the terrors of the **invisible world**', making terror 'the primary principle of religion' (p. 87). Indeed, while it is impossible for people to sustain a state of mind in which they are poised between 'an **eternity** of happiness and an eternity of misery', being in it at all upsets the '**temper**' and leads to the 'gloom and melancholy' that characterizes 'all **devout people**' (p. 87).

Philo concludes by asserting the absurdity of the belief that God requires flattery, or will be in any way offended by human beings making 'the freest use of our reason' (p. 88). If the 'whole of natural theology' amounts only to the proposition, '*That the cause or causes of order in the universe probably bear some remote analogy to human intelligence*', then, unless this proposition can be taken further, it is hard to see how it affects life (p. 88). All it requires is 'philosophical assent', on the grounds that the arguments for it outweigh the objections to it (p. 88). What people understandably long for is some 'particular **revelation**', disclosing God's nature (p. 89). Indeed, the person who is conscious of the limitations of 'natural reason' turns eagerly to revelation (p. 89). Only the 'dogmatist' maintains that philosophical speculation will yield 'a complete **system of theology**' (p. 89). Thus, being a 'philosophical skeptic' is 'the first and most essential step towards being a sound, believing *Christian*' (p. 89).

Having listened to this discussion, Pamphilus' judgement is that '*Philo's* principles are more probable than *Demea's*, but that those of *Cleanthes* approach still nearer to the truth' (p. 89).

Overview

The following section is a chapter-by-chapter overview of the twelve Parts in David Hume's *Dialogues Concerning Natural Religion*, designed for quick reference to the detailed summary above. Readers may also find this overview section helpful for revision.

Pamphilus to Hermippus (pp. 1–2)

The narrator, Pamphilus, explains that, although the dialogue may be out of fashion as a literary form, it is a good way of exploring difficult philosophical issues. He introduces the three protagonists in the *Dialogues*: Cleanthes, the 'accurate' philosopher; Philo, the 'careless' sceptic; and Demea, who upholds 'rigid inflexible orthodoxy'.

Part I (pp. 3–12)

Philo and Demea agree that natural theology is a difficult subject. Philo argues that it is important to recognize the limitations of human reason, particularly in relation to such issues as the origin of the world. However, Cleanthes challenges Philo's professed scepticism. Sceptics claim to doubt all sorts of things, but find it hard to sustain their position, in the face of everyday experience. He maintains that reason has an important role in theological enquiries, and that it will tend to confirm religious beliefs.

Detailed Summary of David Hume's Dialogues

Part II (pp. 13–22)

Demea argues that no one seriously doubts God's existence, but human beings cannot discover anything about God's nature. Philo agrees. God is known only as the cause of the universe; as human beings have no experience of his attributes, they can know nothing about them. Cleanthes dissents, using a version of the **design argument**. Human beings can learn about God's nature, and its resemblance to that of human beings, from the similarity of the world he has designed to objects designed by human beings. However, Philo makes the point that the world's resemblance to, for example, a house is not so close that we are entitled to conclude that they must have similar causes. The fact that the world operates in an orderly and predictable way does not prove that it has an intelligent cause, as this may just be due to the nature of matter. We could only be sure that the universe is designed if we had actual experience of its having come about through design.

Part III (pp. 23–7)

According to Cleanthes, there is no need to prove that the works of nature resemble objects made by human beings, because the resemblance is self-evident. He cites the example of the eye: its structure could only have come about through design.

Part IV (pp. 28–33)

Philo points out that a mental world requires a cause just as much as a material one. Even if the universe has been caused by a supreme mind, that mind would itself require a cause, and so on *ad infinitum*. It would be more economical to say that the universe contained the source of its own order than to say that this order requires God as its cause, but that God does not require a cause. In the case of the universe and God, an attempt is being made to explain a particular effect (the universe) by a particular cause (God), which is no more capable of explanation than the effect.

Part V (pp. 34–8)

Philo turns to further difficulties in Cleanthes' position. If knowledge of God's nature is based solely on the universe, its many defects mean that we cannot be sure that his nature is perfect. Even if the universe were perfect, it might have been made following many bungled attempts, or might be the work of more than one god. All this underlines the advantages of establishing God' perfect nature by *a priori* arguments, rather than *a posteriori* ones, which rely solely on our experience of the world.

Part VI (pp. 39–43)

Cleanthes has maintained that similar effects arise from similar causes, but Philo argues that, as the world resembles an animal more than an object made by human beings, perhaps it is an animal with God as its soul. But, if any one explanation of the world had to be defended, it would be the idea that it is governed by an inherent principle of order. Instead of being amazed that the world operates according to predictable laws of nature, we should recognize that a stable environment would be impossible without them.

Part VII (pp. 44–8)

Philo considers the idea that the universe resembles an animal or vegetable more than an object made by human beings, which suggests that its cause ought to be attributed to generation or vegetation, rather than intelligent design. Demea objects that there is no evidence to support such hypotheses, but this is precisely Philo's point. The limited nature of their experience means that human beings have insufficient evidence to decide which of these hypotheses, if any, is correct. Cleanthes has come down on the side of intelligent design, but experience cannot prove his view to be correct. He would need *a priori* proof that thought and order are inseparably linked.

Part VIII (pp. 49–53)

Philo goes on to say that it is all very well for Cleanthes to claim that the adjustment of the various parts of the body to each other in humans and animals indicates intelligent design, but no animal would survive unless its body parts were so adjusted. Cleanthes' response is to argue that Philo's position does not do justice to such features as eyes and ears, which clearly show that the world has been designed by a benevolent God.

Part IX (pp. 54–7)

Demea claims that *a posteriori* arguments, such those used by Cleanthes, just create problems. It is better to depend on *a priori* ones. Whatever exists must have a cause, so, unless we are prepared to accept an infinite regress of causes, there must be a **first cause**, which cannot be thought not to exist, and this is God. Cleanthes rejects this approach, which combines the **cosmological** and **ontological arguments** for the existence of God. What can be thought to exist can also be thought not to exist. There is no being whose non-existence implies a contradiction, so we can conceive of God as non-existent. Demea's argument also gives no reason for concluding that it is God, not the universe itself, which has qualities that, if known, would make its non-existence seem self-contradictory. Further, it takes no account of the point that, if there is a succession of objects, with each one causing the next, there is no necessity to look for a cause of the succession as a whole.

Part X (pp. 58–66)

Demea suggests that it is human beings' common experience of misery, rather than reason, that makes them believe in God. A stranger, new to the world, would be appalled at all its sorrow and distress. Cleanthes claims that unhappiness is not widespread, but Philo raises the **problem of evil**. Can the resemblance of God's benevolence and mercy to those found in human beings be maintained in the face of human and animal misery? If God is **infinitely powerful** and benevolent, why is there so much natural and moral evil in the world? Cleanthes acknowledges the importance of his point. Religious belief cannot be sustained if all human beings are miserable. For Demea, though, there is no problem: there will be happiness in a future life. Cleanthes dismisses this argument as mere speculation, and insists that the world contains more pleasure than pain. But Philo charges Cleanthes with making the truth of religion depend on a point that cannot be proved one way or the other. How can anybody calculate the balance of pleasure and pain in the world? Moreover, if God is infinitely powerful and benevolent, why is there any pain at all? Certainly, its existence makes it impossible to prove the existence of such a God from the nature of the world.

Part XI (pp. 67–76)

Cleanthes replies that natural evil and moral evil may make it impossible to prove the existence of an infinite God, but it is possible to establish the existence of a finitely perfect one. But Philo argues that, although the suffering in the world may be compatible with its having being designed by a (finitely) good God, we would not conclude, on the evidence of the world alone, that such a God had made it, because it is not the kind of world we would expect him to have made. Philo goes on to list features of the world, such as the inadequacy of human and animal powers, which contribute to suffering. A good God would have created a world with less suffering.

Part XII (pp. 77–89)

Following Demea's departure, Philo appears to change position, professing a deep sense of religion. He acknowledges evidence of design in nature, and accepts that God's existence can be established by reason. He now attacks popular religion, which he considers worse than no religion at all. Cleanthes makes the point that it at least enforces morality, but Philo believes that most people are incapable of believing in the kind of God who requires only virtuous conduct from his followers. Religious groups like to claim that they help to uphold morality, but, if this were the case, society would entrust government to religious leaders, not deny it to them.

Cleanthes sees genuine religious belief as a source of comfort, while Philo thinks that the main emphasis of popular religion is on divine punishment. This is why devout people are often melancholy, although most people only think about such matters when depressed. He rejects the view that God condemns the use of reason in theology, but thinks that the whole of natural theology adds up only to the proposition that there is some resemblance between the cause of the world and human intelligence. Being a sceptic is the first step towards Christian belief, because the philosopher recognizes the limitations of human reason and the need for God to reveal his nature to human beings.

Overall, Pamphilus considers Cleanthes' views to be convincing.

Glossary

Abstract argument. An argument that relies on ideas, as opposed to empirical facts or particular examples. Demea dismisses Cleanthes' arguments for God's existence, because they are based on experience of the world and are not the sort of abstract arguments he puts forward himself.

Abstruse points of theory. A theory that is complex and hard to understand.

Adjustment. Cleanthes claims that the adjustment or adaptation found in the world, such as of one part of the human body to another, proves design.

Analogy/analogical reasoning. Drawing a parallel between two things on the basis of similarities between them. Cleanthes draws an analogy between the world/features of it (such as the eye) and objects made by human beings, and then argues that, as there are similarities between them, they must have similar causes.

Antecedently. previously.

Anthropomorphism/anthropomorphic/anthropomorphite. Making something human-like, expressing it in human form. Both Philo and Demea accuse Cleanthes of being an 'anthropomorphite', because of his human-centred approach to God and the world: as the world so obviously resembles an object made by human beings, its cause, God, must resemble human beings in many respects.

A posteriori. That which comes after, or is based on, experience/ empirical evidence. Cleanthes claims that human beings can establish God's existence and attributes *a posteriori*. However, Philo and Demea reject his argument, because they do not accept the alleged 'experience' on which it is based. They do not agree that the resemblance of the world to an object made by human beings is so close as to warrant the conclusion that they must have similar causes.

Appearances. The way things seem to us, how we understand them to be.

Apprehension(s). In the *Dialogues*, mind(s), ability to understand something.

A priori. That which comes before experience, and which holds (or is claimed to hold) irrespective of experience. Demea claims that human beings can establish God's existence and attributes *a priori*, arguing that everything must have a cause, so, unless we accept an infinite regress of causes, there must be a first cause, which cannot be thought not to exist, and this is God. However, Cleanthes points out the flaws in the argument. Anything that can be thought to exist can also be thought not to exist; therefore, there is no being whose non-existence implies a contradiction; so God can be thought of as non-existent. In a succession of objects, with each one causing the next, there is no necessity to look for a cause of the succession as a whole.

Architect. God is sometimes referred to as the 'architect' of the world. However, Philo argues that, if we see a house, we know that an architect designed it, because we already have experience of architects designing houses, but this is not so with the world and God.

Art (human). Human skill, as in objects that are designed and made by human beings.

Artifice. Skilful design.

Atheist. One who is convinced that there is no God, as opposed to an agnostic, who merely doubts God's existence. In the eighteenth century, few people would have dared to admit to being atheists, whatever their actual views.

Attribute(s). Properties, characteristics. The *Dialogues* focus on God's attributes, such as his power, goodness and mercy, and whether or not experience of the world gives human beings knowledge of these attributes.

Author. Another way of referring to God as the designer or architect of the world.

Being of God. A way of referring to God's nature or attributes.

Benevolent. Wishing to do good. It is an attribute of God, who is believed to wish human beings (his creatures) well, and to care for them. In Christianity, God is believed to be infinitely benevolent.

Blind nature. Nature, which is indifferent to human well-being, as opposed to God, who is believed to be benevolent.

Brahmin. A Hindu priest. Hume refers to Hindu teachings about the origin of the universe.

Cause. That which brings about a certain effect, as in God being the cause of the universe.

Cavils. Fault-finding arguments, baseless objections.

Christianity/Christian. Although concerned with the existence and attributes of a God who is consistent with the Christian concept of God, there is little explicit reference to Christianity in the *Dialogues*.

Cleanthes. One of the three protagonists in the *Dialogues*, described by the narrator, Pamphilus, as an 'accurate' philosopher. He puts forward a version of the design argument, maintaining that it is possible to prove God's existence and nature by the use of reason.

Comforts (of religion). The reassurance religion provides by teaching that a benevolent God made the world and that there is life after death.

Conceive. Think of.

Conjecture. Opinion that is not adequately supported by evidence.

Conjoined. Joined with.

Consolation (of religion). The reassurance religion provides. See also comforts.

Constancy in the forms. The fact that the world operates according to predictable laws and is thus a stable environment. Philo makes the point (against Cleanthes) that, instead of being amazed at this, we should simply recognize that the world would not be habitable, unless it were the case.

Contingent. In the *Dialogues*, the idea that the world and all it contains could not-exist, and can be thought of as not-existing, whereas God (according to Demea) must exist (cannot not-exist), and cannot be thought of as not existing.

Contradiction. Used in an unfamiliar context in the *Dialogues*. According to Demea, God is a being who cannot not-exist; therefore, it is contradictory to say or to think that he does not exist.

Contrivance. Design, invention.

Copernicus, Nicolaus (1473–1543). Scientist who propounded the theory that the earth moves around the sun.

Corporeal. Have a body, physical.

Corrupted. Wicked, depraved.

Cosmogony. Theory(ies) about the cause or origin of the universe.

Cosmological argument. One of the traditional arguments for the existence of God, which argues from the existence of the world and/or how it exists to God as its cause. In his *Summa*

Theologica, St Thomas Aquinas argues (second way or proof of the existence of God) that, as everything has a cause, there must either be an infinite regress of causes or a first cause, and, as there cannot be an infinite regress of causes, there must be a first cause of the world, God; and (third way or proof of the existence of God): the world consists of things that could not-exist (or 'contingent' things); but, if only such things existed, there must have been a time when nothing existed, in which case nothing would exist now; therefore, there must exist a being that cannot not-exist (a being that exists necessarily), God. Demea uses elements of these arguments in his attempted proof of God's existence.

Creation of the universe. The idea that the universe was designed and brought into being by God, rather than coming into existence as the result of natural processes.

Creator. Term applied to God as the maker of the universe. In Christian theology, God made the universe from nothing.

Creature. Something created. If God made the world, human beings are creatures.

Curious. In the *Dialogues*, careful or painstaking.

Damned. Those condemned to hell/eternal punishment by God.

Debtors. Those sent to gaol by their creditors, until they paid their debts. This was a common occurrence in the eighteenth century.

Deduce. In the *Dialogues*, infer or conclude.

Defect(s). The faults or shortcomings of the world, which give rise to human and animal suffering.

Deity. God.

Demea. One of the three protagonists in the *Dialogues*. He is described by the narrator, Pamphilus, as taking a position of 'rigid, inflexible orthodoxy' on religious matters. He does not believe that human beings can discover anything about God's nature through the use of reason, and tries to prove God's existence by *a priori* arguments.

Demonstrable/demonstrate/demonstration. In the *Dialogues*, something capable of being proved conclusively by the use of (arguments derived from) reason, proving something conclusively by the use of (arguments derived from) reason.

Departed souls. The dead.

Design. In the *Dialogues*, the term is used in the context of the issue being discussed: whether or not God designed the universe and whether or not this is can be proved.

Design argument. One of the traditional arguments for the existence of God. Cleanthes puts forward a version of it, pointing to similarities between the world and objects designed and made by human beings, and arguing that, as the effects are similar, the causes must also be similar.

Devout people. Religious people. The term is used rather disparagingly, to refer to the conventionally religious, who are depressed by the prospect of God punishing them for their sins.

Dialogue. Written work presented in the form of conversation.

Dissimulation. Dissembling, being hypocritical. Philo maintains that this is a characteristic of many conventionally religious people.

Divine. Relating to God, or (as in 'Divines') a member of the clergy or someone with expert knowledge of theology.

Doctrine. In the *Dialogues*, religious teaching(s) or belief(s).

Dogmatism. In the *Dialogues*, treating something as true, despite evidence to the contrary.

Elect (the). Those God has chosen for salvation, and who will go to heaven.

Glossary

Empirical. That which relates to, or is based on, experience. Empiricists maintain that experience is human beings' only source of knowledge of the world.

Epicurus (341–270 BC). Greek philosopher. See also problem of evil.

Essence/whole essence (of God). Essential or inner nature (of God).

Eternity. Forever. Those sent to heaven or hell will be there for eternity.

Experience. What relates to the empirical world, and the way that human beings experience things, which some consider to be human beings' only source of knowledge of the world.

Faculties. Powers, powers of the mind.

Faith. In the *Dialogues*, either simply religious belief/belief in God, or trusting belief in God, which is unsupported by clear evidence.

Fecundity. Fertility, rich diversity.

Felicity. Happiness.

Finite. Limited.

Finitely perfect. Cleanthes acknowledges the difficulties of proving the existence of an infinitely perfect God, and so argues that it is possible to prove the existence of a finitely perfect one: for example a God who is powerful and benevolent but not infinitely so. Acceptance of such limitations makes it easier to account for the presence of evil in the world. See also problem of evil.

Fire and brimstone. The torments of hell.

First cause. God, the creator of the universe. See also cosmological argument.

Free thinkers. Those who speculate freely about the existence of God and religious issues (and who may not show consideration for the sensitivities of religious believers).

Frugality. In the *Dialogues*, this refers to the economical distribution of powers to human beings and animals. According to Philo, they would be happier if they possessed greater powers, and this is a reason for rejecting Cleanthes' arguments.

Future worlds. Heaven, a future life in which God will reward the good/those who have suffered in spite of their goodness, and punish the wicked/those who have prospered in spite of their wickedness.

Galileo Galilei (1564–1642). Scientist who made important contributions to physics and astronomy.

General laws. In the *Dialogues*, laws of nature, which make the world a stable environment that operates predictably. However, they also cause suffering, and, according to Philo, provide a reason for rejecting Cleanthes' arguments.

God. The attributes of God, discussed in the *Dialogues*, which include infinite power, benevolence and mercy, are consistent with those of the Christian God, but there is little explicit reference to Christianity or Christian belief.

Hermippus. Receives an account of the *Dialogues* from Pamphilus.

Human reason. Human beings' ability to think, and to draw inferences from evidence, which distinguishes them from animals. In the *Dialogues*, the key issue is the extent to which human reason is capable of discovering God's attributes, with Philo insisting that such knowledge is not attainable, because it is outside human experience.

Hypothesis. A theory put forward as a basis for reasoning, or starting-point for discussion.

Ignorant ages. Earlier periods of history, when free discussion of religious issues was forbidden or discouraged, because of possible damage to religious belief.

Immutability (of God). The idea that God, unlike human beings, is unchanging, and does not have emotions. See also simplicity. This view is challenged by Cleanthes, who feels that, although God possesses attributes which are beyond human understanding, such immutability is inconsistent with God's possessing an intelligent nature, resembling that of human beings.

Impotent. Powerless, unable to accomplish something. Philo argues that God must be impotent, if he wishes to stop evil, but it still exists in the world.

Incomprehensible. In the *Dialogues*, the idea that God's nature/attributes cannot be understood/are beyond human understanding.

In infinitum. Indefinitely, an endless succession of.

Infer/inference. Concluding one thing from something else, as in inferring the existence of a God who, in some respects, resembles human beings from the similarities between the world and objects made by human beings.

Infinite. Unlimited, without limit.

Infinite benevolence. God's benevolence is believed to be unlimited.

Infinite power. God's power is believed to be unlimited, so he is omnipotent.

Infinite succession of causes. Endless sequence of causes (and effects).

Infinite wisdom. God's wisdom is believed to be unlimited.

Inherent. Existing as a natural part of (something). One of Philo's arguments against Cleanthes is that it is more economical to accept that the order we find in the world (the fact that it operates according to predictable laws of nature) is inherent in matter than to insist that it could only have been caused by God.

Intelligent author/cause (of the universe). God, who, according to Cleanthes, has intelligence resembling that of human beings.

Inviolable laws. Laws of nature.

Invisible world. The supernatural world, the world beyond the natural world.

Knitting-loom. In the eighteenth century, an example of sophisticated technology.

Libertine. Immoral person and free thinker.

Locke, John (1632–1704). British empiricist philosopher and author of the *Essay Concerning Human Understanding, Two Treatises of Government* and *The Reasonableness of Christianity*. See also empirical.

Malefactors. Wrongdoers, criminals.

Malevolent. Wishing to do evil. Philo argues that, if God has the power to prevent evil but it still exists in the world, he must be malevolent.

Material world. The physical world.

Matter. That of which the universe consists apart from mind (and spirit). Philo argues that it may have properties that are not perceived by those who insist that only God could have caused the order found in it.

Maxim. Rule of conduct.

Mechanic. In the *Dialogues*, maker of machinery.

Mediums. In the *Dialogues*, methods, arguments.

Mental world. The intellectual world, the world of ideas, as opposed to the physical or material world.

Metaphysical reasoning. Metaphysics is the investigation of what really exists, such as whether or not there is a God or only matter. The problem with metaphysical enquiry (as indicated by Cleanthes' response to Demea's attempts to prove God's existence) is that it considers issues which go beyond ordinary experience, so there is no way of proving the truth or falsity of metaphysical propositions.

Mind. Used to refer to both human minds and to God, the supreme mind who is the cause of the universe.

Model of the whole universe. According to Demea, Cleanthes, by focusing so much on the similarities between the natural world and objects made by human beings, models God on human intelligence, and thus fails to do justice to God's infinite powers.

Moral evil. Human actions that cause suffering, such as violence, torture and theft.

Mysticism/mystic. Direct knowledge of/contact with God. But Cleanthes accuses Demea of mysticism, because he denies that our experience of the world gives us knowledge of God.

Natural religion/theology. What human beings can find out about God through the use of their reason and from experience, without the help of revelation. Cleanthes believes that we can prove God's existence and some of his attributes, such as his benevolence, from our experience of the world.

Natural evil. Natural features of the world that cause suffering, such as diseases, hurricanes and floods.

Nature. In the *Dialogues*, the term refers both to the natural world and to God's nature/attributes.

Necessary existence/necessarily existent. That which exists necessarily (cannot not-exist), as Demea claims God does.

Newton, Isaac (1642–1727). British scientist and mathematician, whom David Hume greatly admired.

Ontological argument. One of the traditional arguments for the existence of God, which argues from the concept of God to his existence. In his *Proslogion*, St Anselm describes God as a being than which none greater can be thought. But if such a being exists only in the understanding, then a greater being can be thought: one that also exists in reality. But this would be contradictory. Therefore, God cannot exist only in the understanding, but must also exist in reality. Further, a being which cannot be thought of as not-existing is greater than a being which can be thought of as not-existing. But if the being than which a greater cannot be thought can be thought of as not-existing, that being is not that than which a greater cannot be thought. And this is contradictory. So God cannot be thought of as not-existing. Demea uses elements of these arguments in his attempted proof of God's existence.

Original intelligence. God.

Orthodox. Generally accepted. Demea is described as having (rigidly) orthodox religious views, so he is likely to reject any novel or unconventional religious ideas.

Pamphilus. Narrator of the *Dialogues*, who does not take part in them.

Pedagogue. Teacher.

Perfection/perfect. Without fault, a quality which is without fault. Philo points out that human concepts of perfect qualities are based on human experience, and so do not enable us to understand God's perfect qualities.

Perpetual motion. Motion that does not cease.

Philo. One of the three protagonists in the *Dialogues*. He is described by the narrator, Pamphilus, as a 'careless' sceptic. He out-argues Cleanthes, and shows that God's existence and nature cannot be proved by the use of reason. In the final chapter, he appears to change position, accepting a weak version of the design argument while emphasizing the importance of revelation.

Philosopher(s). One who studies and practises/teaches philosophy.

Philosophy. Literally, love of wisdom. The study of ultimate reality, what really exists, the most general principles of things.

Piously. Devoutly.

Popular religion. Religion followed, and religious beliefs held, by ordinary, uneducated people, and which, according to Philo, emphasizes fear of divine punishment and hell.

Preservation of individuals/propagation of the species. According to Philo, this is the only purpose that the world seems to have.

Problem of evil. The problem that arises from the apparent contradiction between the presence in the world of natural evil and moral evil and the belief that it was created by an infinitely powerful and infinitely benevolent God. Philo puts Epicurus' question to Cleanthes: 'Is he [God] willing to prevent evil, but not able? then he is impotent. Is he able, but not willing? then he is malevolent. Is he both able and willing? whence then is evil?'

Pyrrhonists. Those who follow Pyrrho of Elis (c. 365–275 BC), a Greek philosopher, who established a profoundly sceptical approach to philosophical enquiry.

Ravishes. In the *Dialogues*, delights.

Received opinions. Orthodox religious beliefs.

Revealed theology. What we can find out/know about God from revelation. See also natural theology.

Revelation. What God chooses to disclose of himself to human beings through, for example, prophets and holy scriptures. See also natural theology.

Sagacity. Practical wisdom.

Scepticism/sceptic. Generally, doubt, or refusing to accept non-empirical sources of knowledge. However, in the *Dialogues*, it also refers to profound or Pyrrhonic scepticism, which questions and doubts everything (see Pyrrhonists), including the evidence of the senses. Cleanthes considers such scepticism to be both unsustainable and unproductive.

Self-evident (truth). Completely obvious. In the *Dialogues*, certain things, such as the existence of God and the similarity of features of the world to objects made by human beings, are claimed to be self-evident.

Simplicity (of God). The idea that God, unlike human beings, does not have different faculties or functions. See also immutability.

Soul of the world. In the *Dialogues*, animating or life-giving principle of the world.

Springs and principles (of the universe). Causal principles (which operate within the universe).

Stoics. School of Greek philosophy, which taught self-control and uncomplaining fortitude in the face of pain and adversity.

Supreme Being. God.

Syllogism. A form of reasoning, in which, from two propositions or premises with a common or middle term, a third can be inferred, from which the common term is absent. Philo gives an example of an incomplete syllogism. The two premises are: Our ideas reach no farther than our experience; we have no experience of divine attributes and operations. We can infer the conclusion: our ideas do not reach to divine attributes and operations.

System of theology. In the *Dialogues*, set of religious beliefs.

Temper. In the *Dialogues*, state of mind, mental balance.

Terrors (of religion). Fear of divine punishment and hell, which, according to Philo, are the dominant themes of popular religion.

Theist. One who believes in God.

Theodicy. In Christian theology, arguments which attempt to reconcile belief in an infinitely powerful and benevolent God, who made the world, with the fact that the world contains evil and suffering.

Theologian(s). One who studies and practises/teaches theology.

Theological inquiries/reasonings. Enquiries into/reasonings about religion, including the issues of God's existence and attributes.

Theology. Setting out the beliefs and teachings of a religion in systematic way; academic discipline concerned with the study of religion/religious beliefs and teachings.

Traditional arguments for the existence of God. See cosmological, design and ontological arguments.

Ultimate cause. God, the ultimate or final cause of the universe. See also cosmological argument.

Unity of the divine nature. The simplicity of God.

Universal cause. God.

Universe. Everything that exists, but, in the *Dialogues*, the term is used interchangeably with world, to denote everything that exists apart from God.

Universe of objects. The material world.

Unknown voluntary agent. God.

Untoward. Troublesome, inconvenient.

Volitions. In the *Dialogues*, God willing that potentially damaging or destructive situations or events in the world become beneficial ones.

Vulgar (the). Ordinary, uneducated people.

Vulgar superstition. False, irrational religious belief, held by ordinary, uneducated people.

Works of nature. Natural objects.

World. Used interchangeably with universe.